How to Pray

Including Prayers by

E. STANLEY JONES

How to Pray

What Prayer Really Is

WHEN the disciples asked Jesus, "Lord, teach us to pray," they uttered one of the deepest and most universal cries of the human heart. For men of all ages have instinctively felt that prayer is the distilled essence of religion. If we know how to pray, we know how to be religious; if not, then religion is a closed book. Where there is no effective prayer life, the heart of religion has ceased to beat and religion becomes a dead body of forms and customs and dogmas.

And yet how few Christians have an effective prayer life! (And this includes many ministers.) If I were to put my finger on the greatest lack in American Christianity, I would unhesitantly point to the need for an effective prayer life among laity and ministers. Kagawa once said to second-generation Japanese Christians on the West Coast: "Your greatest lack is that you do not know how to pray." He saw that their Christianity was anemic and ineffective, because they had not learned the discipline of prayer.

If I had one gift, and only one gift, to make to the Christian Church, I would offer the gift of prayer. For everything follows from prayer.

3

Prayer tones up the total life. I find by actual experience I am better or worse as I pray more or less. If my prayer life sags, my whole life sags with it; if my prayer life goes up, my life as a whole goes up with it. To fail here is to fail all down the line; to succeed here is to succeed everywhere.

In the prayer time the battle of the spiritual life is lost or won. Prayer is not an optional subject in the curriculum of living. It is a required subject; it is *the* required subject. And there is no graduation into adequate human living without prayer.

Perhaps we are all more or less convinced of this viewpoint, but the "how" of prayer is the crux of the difficulty. To try to answer that word "how" is the burden of these articles. I propose to begin at the lowest rung of the ladder so that no one will feel I begin beyond him.

1. Breathe the prayer "Lord, teach me to pray" as you begin the quest for a prayer life. Bathe your very quest in prayer. It may be dim, shadowy, unreal, but this may be the first, tottering step toward spiritual maturity.

2. As you begin your quest, you must hold in mind this background of thought about prayer: *The universe is an open universe.* The old conception of the universe as a closed

4

system, fixed unalterably by natural law, a system in which nothing but foregone conclusions can happen, is a thing of the past. In its place has come a universe where law still reigns, but amid and through those laws are open possibilities, open to initiative and to creative faith. In this world of freedom amid law, just as many things are left open contingent upon the human will—things which will never be done except the human will decides to do them—so there are many things open to prayer that will never be done unless we co-operate with God to do them. It is into this world of freedom and possibility we enter as we enter into prayer.

3. Another thought that may serve as a background: *Prayer is not only the refuge of the weak; it is the reinforcement of the strong.* The idea that only weak people pray is false. The strongest character that ever walked our planet prayed. His first public act was to stand on Jordan's banks, "and as he prayed the heavens were opened." His last public act was a prayer: "Father, into Thy hands I commend my spirit." Between that first and that last act his whole life was saturated with prayer. The Man who changed the world turned to the prayer resource.

Prayer, then, is not merely for the weak, it is the strength of the strong. Is the scientist weak who humbly bends his knees to the facts of nature and lets them take him by the hand and lead him into mastery through obedience?

4. A still further thought we must hold: *Prayer is not bending God to my will, but it is a bringing of my will into conformity with God's will, so that his will may work in and through me.* When you are in a small boat and you throw out a boathook to catch hold of the shore, do you pull the shore to yourself, or do you pull yourself to the shore? Prayer is not bending the universe to your will, making God a cosmic bellhop for your purposes, but prayer is co-operating with the purposes of God to do things you never dreamed you could do. The highest form of prayer is that of Jesus in Gethsemane: "Nevertheless, not my will, but Thy will be done"—not "Thy will be borne" as we often translate it, but "Thy will be *done*"—a cooperating with an outgoing, redemptive will that wills our highest.

5. Another consideration must be held in mind: *Prayer is not an occasional exercise to which you turn now and then; it is a life attitude.* It is the will to co-operate with God in your total life. It is an attitude rather than an act. You cannot expect God to come into the occasional, if you refuse him in the continuous. Therefore, I am not impressed with the slogan:

"There are no atheists in foxholes." If men pray only when in foxholes then prayer is a means of getting you out of a hole—foxholes or other kinds—but no part of a life program. Out of the foxhole the prayer probably takes over on his own and God is dismissed.

6. *Prayer, then, is primarily and fundamentally surrender.* Kagawa was right when, asked to define prayer, he replied: "Surrender." It is a surrender of your purposes, your plans, your will into the hands of God to work them out with him. But surrender does not mean weak negativism.

Prayer is the surrender of the wire to the dynamo, of the flower to the sun, of the student to the processes of education. The Gulf Stream will flow through a straw provided the straw is aligned to the Gulf Stream, and not at cross purposes with it.

You, as an individual, surrender to God and then—shall I say it?—God surrenders to you —his power is at your disposal. You are working with an almighty purpose and an almighty purpose is working with you.

7. *Prayer is secondarily assertion.* After you have surrendered to the will of God, you can assert your will within that will. Huxley once wrote to Kingsley: "Science seems to teach in the most unmistakable terms the Christian con-

ception of entire surrender to the will of God. Science says, Sit down before the facts as a little child, be prepared to give up every preconceived notion, be willing to be led anywhere the facts will lead you, or you will know nothing." That is the first attitude of science—humble surrender to the facts. The second attitude is—bold assertion and an assumption of mastery within those facts.

Two attitudes combine—surrender and assertion. The two have to be together: if you only surrender you are weak; if you only assert you are weak. But if you are surrendered and then assertive, you are really strong. You are going to be a positive creative person because surrendered to the will of God.

You are beginning the adventure of co-operation with God. Prayer is just that—co-operation with God.

The Time and Place for Prayer

Now that we have put a background behind prayer we are probably in a position to take the first positive steps in the art of making the prayer life effective.

1. Begin with the environment, the surroundings in which you are to learn to pray. They should be as favorable as possible. In every home

there should be a shrine, perhaps a place curtained off, into which you can enter to keep your tryst with God. In that little shrine there should be the kind of symbols that will help you achieve the prayer mood. If that shrine cannot be arranged, then go into some place corresponding to "the closet" of which Jesus spoke, where you will be alone without disturbance.

2. Perhaps neither plan is possible. Then make your own shrine by your power of inward withdrawal. Learn to "shut the door" even when amid conditions that would otherwise bring disturbance.

That would mean physical and mental relaxation. It is a psychological fact that you cannot engrave anything of a tense conscious mind. Relaxation is necessary to receptivity. This means that your body should be in a condition in which it is least obtrusive.

Be comfortable, but not slouchy. As you enter the prayer period say to your body: "O body of mine, you may be the vehicle through which God may come to me. Be receptive." And then to each organ: "My brain, you are now in the presence of God. Let go, and listen. He speaks; he penetrates; he heals. Receive, receive." And to the eyes: "My eyes, weary with looking at a distracting world, close, and in-

9

wardly see nothing except him into whose presence you have now come. He touches my eyes and they are rested and calm and single and healed." And to the nerves: "O nerves, intelligence department of my being, strained and torn by living in a world of chaos, I now set you to work on the job of reporting better news. Your God comes—comes with the good news of calm, of poise, of resources, of redemption. Open every cell to that healing, to that calm, to that restoration. Receive, receive, receive."

To your sex life say: "O creative part of me, I surrender you to the creator God. When denied your normal expression in procreation, I know that I sublimate your power into other forms—art, poetry, music, creating new hopes, new souls, new life; I can become creative on another level. So I put you at God's disposal. He cleanses; he redirects." And to the whole body: "He is now in every part, untying knotty nerves in his gentleness, bathing every brain cell with his presence, reinforcing every weak place with his strength, healing all your diseases, co-ordinating all parts and making them into a co-operating whole. Open every door! Give him all the keys."

3. Then say to your soul: "O soul of mine, you are now in the audience chamber of God. You will meet him. He will come. He is com-

ing. Let down all the barriers of your inmost being and welcome him. For he is here—now."

4. Remember that the essence of prayer is found in right relationships with God—not the getting of this thing or that thing. Don't hasten to put things before him for God to grant. Let that go for the moment. As he comes let him put his finger on anything in your life not fully surrendered to his will. If anything is sensitive and not fully frank in his presence bring it up honestly and frankly and look at it. If you see the lines of disapproval in his face, let it go. Otherwise that thing will become a barrier and will block your communion.

5. But if nothing comes up don't conjure up false guilts. Very often we think this conjuring up of false guilts is humility. It is not. God is not petty. He is not going around mote-picking. He wants to see if you are essentially sound and set in the right direction. Don't become condemned over imaginary guilts.

6. For instance, suppose that, while you are praying, your mind wanders. Don't become worried over that. Simply take the wandering thought and make it lead you back to him.

7. But suppose the wandering thought is not quite so innocent; it may be actually impure—some sex thought, for instance. That can be

serious, of course, and can block your communion with him, but only if you harbor and hold the thought. If it is dismissed at once, there is no sin in its coming. Thoughts of sin become sinful thoughts only if entertained and given a seat.

We cannot repeat too much the old statement: "You cannot help the birds flying over your head, but you can help their building nests in your hair." The fleeting thought is not sin; the harbored thought is. I have a little technique of my own in dismissing wrong thoughts: I bat my eyes rapidly. The breaks up the thought, for the batting of the eyes demands attention, calling off the attention from the evil thought and then in the midst of it I pray, "O God, help me." That lets me gain my mental equilibrium and control. You may have to work out your own peculiar technique for controlling thoughts.

8. Suppose the interruption of your meditation is not from within by straying thoughts, but from without by disturbing events or persons. Don't let that upset you. Use the interruption. When Jesus went across the lake to get away from the multitudes in order to pray, the people ran around, and when he arrived for his prayer hour there were the crowds again. Instead

of being angered and upset, "out of pity for them he proceeded to teach them at length." (Mark 6:34, after Moffatt.) After feeding them, "he dismissed the crowd, and after saying good-by to them, he went up into the hills to pray" (46). An interruption became an interpretation.

If you are interrupted, let the interruption be not an irritation, but an interpretation. But at the end come back to the prayer period as Jesus did. Don't let the interruption keep you permanently from the prayer time. The season of prayer will be richer for the mastery of the interruption, and the interruption will be richer because of the prayer period.

Almost the whole of Jesus' life was one interruption after another, but he didn't muddle those interruptions. He mastered them and made them contribute to the central purposes of his life. The spirit of his interrupted prayer went into the interruption and made it illustrate his essential spirit.

It may be that you can glory in interruptions as giving opportunity to "evangelize the inevitable." The mosaic of happenings is made into a Christian pattern by the prayer spirit. For prayer is not only an act; it is an attitude. The interrupted prayer act can be perpetuated in the prayer attitude during the interruption.

9. Suppose the prayer period is not interrupted from without or from within, but is simply dull and dry and unreal. That, too, should not upset you. There come such dry, dead emotional periods in every married life, but that needn't disturb the fundamental joy of marriage. The fact is still there intact, although the glow of it may be absent. Hold steady, the glow will return to your prayer hour. Don't give it up because there is no glow.

Pray by the clock if you cannot pray by the heartbeat. In doing so you will be fixing a prayer habit, even if you don't feel a prayer glow. The habit is getting into your nerve cells and is becoming a fixed attitude. That fact is more important than the glow. For, once the habit is fixed, the person is inwardly set for prayer as a life attitude.

Something is happening to you even amid the lack of the sense of reality, for you are being fashioned into a person who lives by principles rather than pulse-beats, by decisions rather than by delights. Prayer is always right, with or without an emotional content. If you cannot pray by an inward click then pray by the outward clock.

Admit of no exceptions in the prayer schedule for the exception will break down the habit. The habit is the important thing.

14

The Steps of Prayer

We are now ready to take the actual steps of prayer, and there are about nine of them.

First, decide what you really want. The "you" is important. It must not be a vagrant part of you wandering into the prayer hour with no intention of committing yourself to your prayer request. You cannot pray with a part of yourself and expect God to answer, for he hears what the whole of you is saying. "In the day that Thou seekest me with the whole heart, thou shalt be found of me." God can only give a whole response to a whole request from a whole person.

Note that Jesus often asked of a supplicant, "What do you want that I should do unto you?" This is vital, for often a sick person asks to be well, when down underneath he wants no such thing. He is using that illness or complaint as a life strategy to gain attention and attendance.

At a family gathering held periodically an aunt used to come regularly, but she always came ill. The rest of the family buzzed around her in sympathy and service. Although ill, she always managed to eat her portion of the big family dinner. There was no doubt that she made the illness her device for drawing attention to herself.

The same thing can happen in the realm of

our moral and spiritual life. We pray with a portion of our beings for moral and spiritual victory. St. Augustine, before he became a saint, used to pray, "O God, make me pure, but not now." Before I was converted, very often I would pray for God to make me good, really afraid that he would take me at my word. Actually, I didn't want to be good. So my prayers were never answered, until in a crisis moment, I really wanted to be different! Then God heard and delivered me, and only then.

Perhaps you are willing that you pray with the whole "you," but the other "you" is not cooperative. Then tell God you are willing to be made willing. Offer your unwillingness to God and with your consent, he will make it into willingness.

> Longing I sought Thy presence, Lord,
> With my whole heart did I call and pray,
> And going out toward Thee, I found Thee,
> Coming to me on the way.

When you see him coming to you on the way you will find that he is more than half way to you.

Here is the experience of a woman who said in the beginning of our conversation, "We have everything in our home—everything and nothing." Now she has something. She says: "My day pivots around or radiates from the quiet hour. I had a miserable time establishing it. I could not control my thoughts and pray. Why, I couldn't offer a sane prayer. I even felt for a time that I was doing myself an injustice to keep trying. Then I confined that time to reading my Bible and writing God a letter. In these letters I am stripped of my self-will, and his will prevails. It is so satisfying, I am trying to catch up on back correspondence. I tell this to you, but if I intimated this to some of my associates, I doubtless would be judged insane. But, if this is insanity, I readily confess I love it."

But there is a beautiful sanity in the procedure, for that woman is used to expressing herself clearly in letters. She transferred the habit to her dealings with God. Note that she says: "In them I am stripped of self-will and his will prevails." The whole person is beginning to talk to God in those letters.

Second, decide whether the thing you want is a Christian thing. God has shown us in Christ what the divine character is like. God is Christ-like. He can only act in a Christ-like way. He cannot answer a prayer that would not fit in with his character.

A woman who was having some illicit relationships with a married man said: "I thought God was going to answer my prayers and give him to me." But how could God do that? She had merely read her desires into the heavens, and the answer was only the echo of her own desires. Her whole wrong moral universe fell to pieces, and she emerged out of it chastened and disillusioned. God cannot reverse the moral universe which is an expression of his moral nature to answer a selfish or immoral whim.

Let us sit down and ask about all our prayers: "Is the thing I want a Christian thing?" And remember that, if it is not a Christian thing, it would do us no good if we got it, for only the Christian thing is the thing that is good for us. Ask God to cleanse your prayers as well as you. For prayer is the naked intent stretching out to God.

Jesus said, "If ye shall ask anything in my name"—that is, in my character, according to my spirit—"that will I do." Within the limits of the character of Christ, which means within the limits of the moral universe, you are free to ask anything and God is free to give you anything.

Third, write it down. The writing of the prayer will probably help you in self-committal. For, if you write it, you will probably mean it. Committing a thing to writing is almost destiny to me; I can hardly change it afterward. The writing of it will also save you from hazy in-

18

definiteness. You will be praying for this and not something else. There will come a time, of course, when you may not need to write things down, for they will have written themselves in you. You can then trust yourself to pray the Christian thing, but at the start it is well to use all the outer helps you can.

There are some who practice the method of writing down their sins and their failures, and then solemnly burning them in a fire as a symbol that the old self and its ways are burned up in the fire of God's love.

Whether it is the motive of getting rid of something, or the motive of getting something, it is well to write it down to clarify it.

Fourth, still the mind. The stilling of the mind is a step in receptivity. Prayer is pure receptivity in the first stage. "As many as *received* him, to them gave he power." If you come to God all tense, you can get little. Let down the bars. They are all on your side; there are none on his.

Receptivity is the first law of the spiritual life. It is the first law of all life. An organism can give out as much as it takes in and no more. If it hasn't learned to receive, it hasn't learned to live. The radiant soul mentioned above says: "God has done more for me in this one year that I have been receptive than I have done

19

for myself in all the years of my life. The stupidity of people who live in a shell!"

In that period of stilling the mind I find myself saying over and over: "Oh, God, you've got me." And again and again the answer comes back: "I know it, my son." Then there is quiet absorptive rest in which you breathe into every fiber if your being the healing grace of the Father himself.

The first thing is to get God. If you get him, everything else follows. I seldom ask for things, for if I have him, I know I'll get all I need in addition. The stilling of the mind is to allow God to get at you, to invade you, to take possession of you. He then pours his very prayers through you. They are his prayers—God-inspired, and hence God-answered.

Whenever I am about to speak I ask the audience to bow their heads in silent prayer. In that silence I always repeat my verse. "Ye have not chosen me, but I have chosen you and ordained you that you should go and bear fruit and that your fruit should remain; that whatsoever ye ask of the Father in my name, he may give it you." The stilling of the mind by the repetition of that verse makes it receptive. I am living in the passive voice. Preaching then is not eager straining, it is receptivity ending in release. The speaker is no longer a reservoir with just so much to give; he is a channel attached to unlimited resources.

The stilling of the mind reminds you not of your pitiful little store, but of the fact that you are now harnessing yourself to God's illimitable fullness.

Prayer is like the fastening of the cup to the wounded side of a pine tree to allow the rosin to pour into it. You are now nestling up into the side of God—the wounded side, if you will—and you allow his grace to fill your cup. You are taking in the very life of God.

"Be still and know," and you will be full. Be unstill and you will not know; you will remain empty.

Using the Prayer Ladder

In our use of a prayer ladder we came in our last article to the step—Still the Mind. The stilling of the mind creates receptivity, and receptivity is the first law of life. Learn that and you know how to live; fail to learn that and you have failed to live.

Now you are ready for the fifth step: *Talk with God about it.* Note I say, "Talk with God," not "Talk to God," for it is a two-way conversation. And the most vital part may be not what you will say to God, but what God will say to you. For God wants not merely to answer your prayer. He wants to *make* you—to make you into the kind of person through whom he can habitually answer prayer. So this prayer episode is part of a process of God-training. God will answer the prayer provided it will contribute in the long run to the making of you.

When you talk with God about it, set the prayer in the light of that general purpose of God to make you the best instrument of his purpose he can make of you. He may have to say a lesser "no," in order to a higher "yes." On the other hand, this prayer may be a part of that higher purpose. If so, then you can talk it over with him with confidence. A boldness will take hold of your spirit as you wait in his presence.

A few mornings ago I awoke at four o'clock coughing my lungs out. I had tried to stagger through an impossible schedule while just skirting pneumonia. That morning hour seemed decisive one way or the other. I grew desperate and bold and clutched the garment of God and held on and said, "O God, I don't ask for many things. I've wanted you more than things, but I am asking for this. If you don't help me, I'm done for. I can't go on. Help me."

I knew that prayer moment had registered. The tide turned. As was said in many a Scripture episode, "He began to amend from the very hour."

Talk with God about it and talk with him in the confidence that he is aching to answer that prayer for you, if it is in line with his general purposes for you.

There is a sixth step: *Promise God what you will do to make this prayer come true.* Since the conversation is a two-way affair, the accomplishment is also two-way. You and God answer it together.

At this point be silent to hear God again, and see if he makes any suggestions to you about your part in answering the prayer. If definite suggestions come to you, then promise that you will carry them out.

For instance, one morning I prayed that Gandhi might not be allowed to die—to die pleading the freedom of his country. Immediately, as I became quiet, I saw that I could send a wire to the President urging him to intervene and mediate. This article was laid aside for a moment to send that wire.

The impulses that come out of the prayer hour are usually true impulses of the Spirit. Some would say these impulses are of the spirit. But those of us who try this two-way living know that you cannot tell where your spirit ends and his Spirit begins. They are now flowing back and forth into each other.

The Spirit stimulates our spirit into Spirit-led activities. "Who caused his glorious arm to go to the right hand of Moses." When Moses lifted his arm God lifted his—their arms worked together —and what a working together!

Therefore, in the silence tell God what you will do to make the prayer come true.

Seventh: *Do everything loving that comes to your mind about it!* This step is important, for it is a cleansing and clarifying step. The word "loving" is important. It is the password to find the source of the suggestions that come to your mind. If the suggestion is not loving, it is probably from your subsconscious mind, and not from the Spirit. The first fruit of the Spirit is "love," and if the suggestion does not fit in with love then don't do it. Wait for the suggestion that does fit in.

If the word "loving" is important, so is the word "do." If you only will to do something and never actually do it, then you will find that God cannot "do." He can only will, awaiting your doing. Your doing looses the floodgates of God's doing.

Eighth: *Thank God for answering in his own way.* God will answer that prayer. No prayers are unanswered. But he may answer "no," as

24

well as "yes." "No" is an answer, and it may really be next in order leading on to a higher "yes."

Moreover, the answer may be delayed in order to toughen your fibre. The very persistence in asking for something over a long period may be one of the most character-toughening processes imaginable. The prayer becomes fixed in a life attitude, and it may be the organizing principle around which life revolves. God may be more concerned that the prayer be there than that the answer be forth-coming. He often holds us off to deepen our characters, so that we will not be spiritual "cry babies," if we do not get everything we want and get it at once.

There is a ninth step: *Release the whole prayer from your conscious thinking.* Don't keep the prayer at the center of your conscious thinking. It may become an anxiety-center. Let it drop down into the subconscious mind and let it work at that greater depth. Then there will be an undertone of prayer in all you do, but there will be no tense anxiety. Dismissing it from the conscious mind is an act of faith that, having committed it to God you leave it in his hands, believing he will do the best thing possible.

One or two thoughts may be helpful in closing this series of brief studies on the practice of prayer:

Prayer is not so much an act as an attitude. The first Beatitude says: "Blessed are the renounced in spirit for theirs is the kingdom of God." The renounced, the surrendered in spirit have what? The kingdom of God! They do not merely belong to the kingdom of God, but the kingdom of God belongs to them! All of its resources are behind them, they work with almighty power. Therefore, they go beyond themselves in thinking, in acting, in accomplishment. They are ordinary men doing extraordinary things.

"The Acts of the Apostles" could be called "The Acts of the Holy Spirit," for the Holy Spirit was taking ordinary human nature and heightening powers and insights until ordinary human nature was quite extraordinary. "My powers are heightened by my God," exclaims Miriam in her song. And that is literally true. There are no limits to what a man will do who does not limit God in his life.

Prayer is opening the channels from our emptiness to God's fullness, from our defeat to his victory.

Therefore, pray or be a prey—a prey to your impulses, to the last happening, to your surroundings. The man who prays overcomes everything, for he is overcome by the most redemp-

26

tive fact of the universe, the will of God. To find that will and live by it is to find yourself. Prayer then makes the most absolutely free man this universe knows. The man who does the will of God actually does his own deepest will.

Prayers by
E. Stanley Jones

Walking with the Lights
Prov. 22:8; 20:17; 10:2, 9

O God, my Light, I looked for Thee in the sky. Thou art there, but I see Thou art here too, in the very nature of things. Help me to walk with Thy green lights. Forgive me that I have walked against Thy redlights. I thought I was only hurting Thee. I was hurting myself, too. *Amen.*

The Kingdom of God Is Among You
Luke 10:27-37

My Father, I see that Thou art Father to Thy family. Thou hast made me so that I cannot get along with myself without getting along with the rest of the family. I see I must live by love or live by loss. Help me this day to live by love. *Amen.*

The Kingdom Works as Self-Frustration
James 3:16-18; 4:1-3; Phil. 3:19

O God, I begin to feel a sense of personal and collective guilt. We have been trying to live against the universe and not with it, and now we are up against it. I'm up against it—we all are. I lift pleading hands to Thee to help me, save me. *Amen.*

Picking Out a Hypothesis
Matt. 6:24; Josh. 24:15; Deut. 30:15-20

O God, I see, I have to choose. I would shrink from that responsibility and lay it over on Thee. But I can't. I must stand up and choose. Help me to make the right choice, take the right way. For the future—Thy future and my future—is in this hour of choice. Help me to choose aright. *Amen.*

How God Reveals Himself
Ps. 19:1-6; Heb. 1:10-12; 2:6-9

O God, I begin to see that Thou art coming to me in Christ. He seems to be that personal approach from the Unseen to me. I would not block that approach. I want Thee, O God, nothing less than Thee. Art Thou, O Christ, God coming to me, that I may come to Thee? Then receive me, for I receive Thee. *Amen.*

God Is My Adventure
Heb. 1:1-3; John 1:1-5, 17-18; Heb. 12:1-2

O Christ, I am so grateful that Thou art God near at hand, God bending to my need. I cannot scale the heavens to find Thee, for I am mired in my own fears and sins. Thou dost come to me. And now there is response within me. I come to Thee! I thank Thee that I come. *Amen.*

32

Fastening on Dead Branches
Matt. 27:3-5; Acts 5:1-5
O God, the hesitancies within me make me want to fasten upon some compromise, some halfway measure. Save me from this. I want nothing less than Thee. I know that anything less than Thee will ultimately let me down. I come to Thee. *Amen.*

Taking the Whole Cross
Rom. 6:2, 5-6, 11-14
O God, I have put my hand to this plow, and I do not intend to look back. I am going all out for Christ. This shall be no halfway business. I shall take the whole cross and not ask for a half cross. Help me to cut loose. In Jesus' name. *Amen.*

The Morning Quiet Hour
Mark 1:35-36; Acts 10:9; Eph. 6:18; I Thess. 5:17
O God, I need Thy silences just as I need physical food. I dedicate myself to them. May I resolve to cut my physical food each time I cut my spiritual intake. Thus soul and body will go up and down together. For I am resolved to see this through and to pay the price to do it. *Amen.*

33

Help Me to Help
Rom. 8:1-2; II Cor. 3:16-18; Gal. 5:1

O God, my Father, how can I express the gratitude my happy soul would tell? "O for a thousand tongues to sing my great Redeemer's praise." Now help me to tell my gratitude not merely in ecstatic praise, but in quiet ways of human helpfulness. Help me to help the next person I meet, and so on through this day. *Amen.*

My I Seem Different
I Cor. 6:9-11; I Pet. 1:8-9; Rom. 8:15-17

O God, I have come into a new world, for a new world has come into me. Help me to live so that people will seem different to me and I seem different to them. For I am different. And I am so grateful. Thank you, Father. *Amen.*

Seeing Our Enemies
Gal. 5:19-21; Matt. 15:19-20; II Tim. 3:2-5

O God, I thank Thee that I see my enemies. I have brought the hidden ones into the light. They are many, and they attack me in subtle, unseen ways. But I am not dismayed. If sin abounds, Thy grace doth much more abound. In that confidence I face them all, expecting Thee to give me nerve and courage and strength to down them one by one—or perhaps all at once. *Amen.*

Made for Loyalty to God
Matt. 9:20-22; Mark 10:51-52; Rom. 8:11

O God, can my lungs do without air, my eyes do without light, my heart do without love, my aesthetic nature do without beauty, my conscience do without truth? No more can I do without Thee, Thou Life of my life, Thou Soul of my soul. I belong to Thee as glove to hand. *Amen.*

Rooted in Thee
Eph. 2:12-22

O God, only those rooted in Thee, the Eternal, can stand up under life. They can take it. I, too, would be able to take it. Then let all my being be rooted in Thee—my thoughts rooted in Thy thoughts, my emotions rooted in Thy love, my will rooted in Thy will. Then shall I live. *Amen.*

Self-Centered Is Self-Disrupted
James 2:8-9; Rom. 12:3, 10, 16; 13:9-10

O God, my Father, I see that Thou hast wrought Thy laws into the texture of my being. How foolish for me to run against those laws and think I can get away with my folly! For I cannot get away with myself. Forgive me the folly of warring with myself and hence with Thee. *Amen.*

Lift Me Out of Myself
Matt. 25:24-25; II Tim. 4:10; I Tim. 6:6-10

O God, I see I cannot center on myself without that self going to rack and ruin. I would present this self of mine to Thee. Lift me out of myself into Thyself, that there I may find my freedom and myself. For Thy will is my home. *Amen.*

My Destructive Self
Matt. 7:1-5; I John 3:17-21

My Father, I see that this imperious, demanding self, like the camel's nose inside the tent, will soon put me out of this earthly habitation. I shall soon not be able to live with it—unless I give it back to Thee for cleansing, for adjustment, for a new basis of living. I do. *Amen.*

I Look to Christ
John 12:5; Matt. 16:15; 26:16, 23, 25; 27:3, 5

Thou Living Christ, I do look to Thee. To whom else can I go? for Thou hast the words of eternal life—of eternal life not only in the hereafter, but in the here and now. And so I look to Thee with eyes of faith, and I take from Thee the power, the release, the victory I so deeply need. And I take it now. *Amen.*

Tempests of Emotion
Mark 9:33-35; Ps. 34:5; Isa. 45:22

O God, I do not sail calm seas. I am driven by tempests of emotion. Help me to harness these to the purposes of Thy Kingdom, for unharnessed they drive me to the rocks upon which both I and my relationships are broken. I surrender myself and my emotions to Thee. *Amen.*

To See Myself Truly
Mark 3:5; Ps. 95:10; Eph. 4:30; Prov. 8:3; Ps. 97:10

O God, give me clear insight and courage to see myself truly, for I may be cloaking my resentments with garments of piety, and I know these resentments are deadly in whatever form they gain a footing in my life. I would harbor no dangerous Trojan-horse enemies within me. Help me then to be completely honest with myself. *Amen.*

Save Me from Clinging Resentments
Gen. 49:7; Eccles. 7:9; Col. 3:8

O God, my Father, I see that good will brings harmony and peace and effectiveness, and that ill will makes for disharmony, upset, and ineffectiveness—it lays a paralyzing hand on soul and body. Then save me from any clinging resentments. Help me to pull them up by the roots. *Amen.*

Anger Is Poison
Ps. 37:8; Eccles. 7:9; Col. 3:8; Prov. 16:32

O God, I see that I pass on to my body the health and unhealth of my mind and soul. I want, then, to be healthy in soul and in mind. Therefore I would take into my very being the health of Thy mind. Let me be saturated with Thy ways and Thy thought that I may live in radiant health through and through. *Amen.*

Forgiving for Christ's Sake
Luke 6:37; 23:34; Eph. 4:31-32; Matt. 18:21-35

O God, the wrong has entered deep into my spirit. In my own strength I cannot forgive. But I am willing to be made willing. Take my willingness and add Thy power, and then I shall be able to forgive. For through Thee I can do anything— yes, anything; even this. *Amen.*

Loving the Unlovely
Luke 22:32; Matt. 5:25-26; Gal. 6:1-2; II Cor. 2:7

O God, I come to Thee to gain understanding sympathy. I am resentful because I don't understand. Give me clear insight and sympathy that I may read in the lives of others the things that make them unattractive to me. And when I understand, help me to forgive. For Jesus' sake. *Amen.*

Help Me Forgive Graciously
Matt. 11:25-26; Luke 6:37; 17:3-4; Eph. 4:32

O God, my Father, nothing that anyone can do against me compares with what I have done against Thee. Thou hast forgiven me—help me to forgive others. And help me to forgive graciously, not grudgingly, for Thou hast forgiven me so graciously. For Jesus' sake. *Amen.*

I Fear the Fear
Prov. 14:27; 19:23; Luke 21:26; Heb. 2:15

O God, I fear the fear that gets rootage in my life. I am anxious about the anxiety that infects me. I am worried about the worry. Give me deliverance from them. Help me to complete freedom from any cramping inhibition and fear. *Amen.*

Fashioned for Faith, Not for Fear
Ps. 37:1, 7-8; Job 3:25; John 14:1, 27

O God, my Father, I see that in my inmost being I am made for confidence and trust and not for worry and anxiety. Thou hast fashioned me for faith and not for fear. Help me then to surrender to what I am made for—faith. Let me this day walk forth in confident faith, afraid of nothing. In Jesus' name. *Amen.*

Home-Grown Fears
Luke 8:26-31; Pss. 31:13; 53:5

O God, our Father, we have filled Thy world and our hearts with fears—needless, devastating fears. Help us, we pray Thee, to find release from these fears and power over them, for they are not our real selves—they are an importation. In Jesus' name. *Amen.*

The Will to Be Well
Luke 8:50; 18:4; 18:41-42; John 5:6; 4:49-53

My Father, I cannot will to be well unless I am reinforced at the center of my being. For I am inwardly flabby. Help me, then, to take the strength of Thy will into the weakness of my own. In Jesus' name. *Amen.*

Unfaced Foes
John 16:33; I John 5:4-5; Isa. 41:10; 43:5

O God, my Father, I have closed my heart to Thy healing and to Thy deliverance. I have wrapped myself within myself—afraid of salvation! I have protected my lungs—from air. My heart—from love! My aesthetic nature—from beauty! Myself—from Thee! Forgive me. *Amen.*

Relax in His Presence
Pss. 55:6; 16:9; Isa. 11:10; Zeph. 3:17

My Father God, I've burned up my soul and body and mind energy in the false energy of fear and worry. Such tenseness has taken me nowhere, except deeper into the mire. Help me this day to link all my energies to the calm of Thy purposes and to the peace of Thy power. Then I shall know harmony and accomplishment. *Amen.*

My Faith, Plus Thine
Prov. 1:33; 3:23-26; Isa. 30:15; 33:24

My Father, I begin to see that my poor faith alone is not all that is left to battle with life's sorrows and troubles. I have a faith, plus Thine. And that "plus" is enough and more than enough. I will work life no longer on the unit principle, but on the cooperative plan. I am no longer afraid —not with Thee. *Amen.*

I Can Do What I Can't
Ps. 23

O living Christ, I see that life is communion—a union with Thee. Not merely in the quiet segregated moments, but in the moments of stress and strain and toil. I now see I can be the happy warrior, for I am drawing heavily on Thy power and going forth in Thy confidence. I can actually do what I can't. I thank Thee, I thank Thee. *Amen.*

Healed to Heal
I Cor. 15:57-58; Phil. 2:12-13; Rom. 15:1-3

O God, Thou art healing me in order to make me a center of healing. This precious gift I hold within my hand, not to gaze at in joyful reverence, but to pass it on. Freely I have received; help me freely to give. In Jesus' name. *Amen.*

The Fear of Failure
Isa. 55

My Father, I've been afraid of failure. In fear of failure the self still lurks, afraid of what others will say. Forgive me that I've looked at the verdict of others, instead of at the verdict of Thy "Well done," as through failure and success I've been true to Thee. O help me to be true—I care for naught else. *Amen.*

Confident in Thy Confidence
Rom. 12:8; Prov. 15:13-15; 17:22

Thou confident God, going steadily on amid the deflections and betrayals of men, help me to have Thy patience and Thy confidence. For from now on I'm eternally linked with Thee. When Thou dost fall, I shall—until then, I stand. Glory be! *Amen.*

The Way of Reality
I Cor. 8:1; Rom. 11:33; John 1:17; 8:32

O God, my Father, I see that amid all the ways of men Thou hast a way—the way that is written into the nature of reality. Help me to find that way that I may live, for I cannot fumble this business of living. Time is too short, and living too serious. In Jesus' name. *Amen.*

Relaxing in Thy Presence
Pss. 4:4-5; 34:8; 36:7; 91:1-2

O God, I enter now a life of complete frankness and open honesty. I live with no hidden, closed caverns in the depths of me. I am from now on "a child of light," and know no secrets withheld, no sore points suppressed. I am to be simple and unaffected—and Thine. *Amen.*

I Am Free Indeed
Heb. 12:1-2; Isa. 45:22; John 3:14-16

O my Lord and Master, I see that I can be free only when I am in love with Thee, for love of Thee is love of myself. What bondage—what freedom! I know now what the promise means when it says, "If the Son shall make you free, ye shall be free indeed." I am free indeed. I thank Thee, Father. *Amen.*

What I Am Without Sham
II Cor. 8:11-12; I Cor. 1:26-29; 3:21-23
O God, I want to be what I am without any
sham. But I want to be more: I want to be the man
Thou dost intend me to be. Then I shall stand
with simplicity and dignity in Thy will and purpose. For everything in Thy will is great—perhaps
I shall be great, too, if I stay in Thy will. In Jesus'
name. *Amen.*

Save Me from Make-Believe Strengths
Rom. 12:3, 16; 14:1, 4, 10, 13, 15
O God, I come to Thee to find power to be
really strong. Save me from these make-believe
strengths that leave me weak. I want to be the
kind of person nothing without can upset, for
I am so sure within. But only as I am inwardly
fortified by Thy strength can this happen. I ex-
pose myself to Thy true strength. *Amen.*

I Belong to Victory
Heb. 10:38-39; Acts 13:13; Gal. 2:11-13
My God and Father, I belong to Thee, Thou
Creator God. I would link myself with Thy Creative Spirit and become creative and positive and
victorious. For I belong to today and tomorrow
and forever. I do not belong to a wistful sighing
over a dead past, nor to a fear of today—I belong
to victory! Help me take it. *Amen.*

44

Confidence and a Song
Gal. 5:1; II Tim. 1:7; John 6:66-68
Thou frank and openhearted Christ, help me to
be frank and openhearted, for I want to be adequate
and contributive. Take from my life all negative
thinking, all refusal to accept responsibility, all
fearful attitudes, and let me face life with a
confidence and with a song. In Jesus' name. *Amen.*

To Will Thy Will
Gal. 2:21; II Tim. 3:16-17; 4:10-11; Phil. 4:13
O God, Thou who willest that I will, help this
will of mine to will Thy will. Help me to link
my littleness to Thy greatness, my faintheartedness
to Thy loving aggression, my holding back to Thy
ongoingness, my fear to Thy faith—then nothing
can stop me. *Amen.*

I Cannot Be Inferior
II Cor. 9:8; Eph. 2:19-22; Rev. 19:10; Jer. 1:6-10
My Father, in Thee how can I be a worm of
the dust? I'm not. I'm Thy child, made in Thine
image, enforced by Thy mind, empowered by
Thy purposes, rekindled by Thy love, and re-
made by Thy redemption. I cannot be inferior
since Thou art not, for I am in Thee. *Amen.*

All I Can Be
Rom. 12:3-8; I Cor. 3:18-23; 6:19-20

O God, stretch me to my utmost—and that utmost means all I can be in and through Thee; but don't let me cry for the moon. Help me to evaluate what I can be in Thee, and then let me go out for that goal with all I have and with all Thou canst give to me. In Jesus' name. *Amen.*

What I Have Is Thine
Matt. 9:29; 17:20; Mark 11:22; Rom. 14:23; Mark 11:24

O God, in Thee I cannot be defeated or fail, for I am now under a living mind and a living will, and the future is open. I haven't much to offer, but what I have is Thine. Heighten these powers, so that I shall be a continuous surprise, even to myself. *Amen.*

In Thee I Gaze and Grow
Gal. 5:16, 24-25; Rom. 13:14; Eph. 3:14-21

O God, I dare not gaze on myself, even in Thee. But I do gaze on Thee and find myself. In Thee I gaze and grow—in myself I cultivate and deteriorate. So now my eye is getting in focus. I begin to understand what Thou didst mean: "If thine eye be single, thy whole body shall be full of light." My whole body is full of light. Thank Thee, Father. *Amen.*

Thou Homeland of My Soul
Eph. 1:17-23; Phil. 4:8-9

My Father, God, I see where I should be centered—Thou art my center and my circumference. In Thee I am safe and steady and growing. In sickness and sin and myself, I wither. For I am fashioned in my inmost being for Thee—Thou Homeland of my soul. I thank Thee. *Amen.*

Giving All, I Take All
Matt. 5:1-10; Luke 18:16-17

O God, it seems too good to be true—that all these powers are mine! Mine? I, who have been defeated and negative and afraid; can I dare take all these powers of victory and release and usefulness? Then I do take them, for I keep nothing back—absolutely nothing. And, giving all, I take all. In Jesus' name. *Amen.*

Let Me Breathe Thee
John 1:12-13; 15:1-18

O God, Thou who dost wrap me round as the atmosphere wraps my body round, let me respond to Thee as my physical body responds to its environment and lives. Let me breathe Thee now—deep breaths of Thee; let me receive Thee into every pore and fiber of my being. Help me to live by Thee—then I shall live. *Amen.*

47

Necessary to Thee
II Cor. 6:1-10; Rom. 8:13-14

O God, am I—I, who thought myself inferior—necessary not only to others, but to Thee? Then help me never to let Thee down. Help me humbly to receive from Thee and humbly to give back to Thee—a two-way traffic with Thee! I shall grow as I get and give. I thank Thee. *Amen.*

I Am Yet Weak
John 16:32; Matt. 28:19-20; 14:16-21

O God, You and I will work this out together. I am yet weak and can take only a small part of the load—You'll have to take the heavy end. But You have my will and, when it develops, You'll have my strength, too. I thank Thee. *Amen.*

Convert My Handicaps
II Cor. 10:10; 11:6; 12:7-12

My Father, what I lack by nature I shall make up by grace. I cannot draw heavily on many things, but I can draw heavily on Thee. Make my very weaknesses into Thy strength. Help me to take hold of my handicaps and convert them into handiwork. In Jesus' name. *Amen.*

Compel Me to Flee—Forward
Acts 5:40-42; Phil. 1:12-19; I Pet. 4:14

My Father and my God, I see that my life will be made or broken at the place where I meet and deal with my obstacles. Help me not to run away from them, but to run toward them, to tackle and overcome them. Help me to take the impulse to flee and compel it to make me flee forward. In His name. *Amen.*

Quicken Me to Creativity
I Cor. 1:27-28; 6:9-11; Philem. 10-16

O Christ, Thou creator of living thoughts in dead brains; Thou stimulator of living love in petrified hearts; Thou arouser of living action in decayed wills; Thou giver of life, I ask Thee to enter into me and to stimulate and quicken every fiber and nerve cell that I too may become creative. *Amen.*

Thy Laws Are Thy Loves
I Cor. 6:12-20

My Father, I see that Thy school is strict, but the end is redemption. Thy laws, however uncompromising, are our salvation. They are made for us, and they mean to make us. Help us then not to chafe at them as enemies, but to embrace them as friends. For all Thy laws are Thy loves. I thank Thee. *Amen.*

I Shall Die on No Trifling Cross
Rom. 15:1-2; 1:24; II Cor. 5:15; Phil. 2:4

O Christ—I understand. The whole meaning of life is made plain. I am to follow Thee to no trifling cross, but to this decisive cross on which I shall die—die to my own futile self-will in order to live to Thy will; die to my own petty self in order to live to Thy free and strong self. Help me then from this moment to discipline my life to Thy will. *Amen.*

I Offer My Sex Powers to Thee
Jude 16, 18-21; Eph. 2:1-3; Rom. 8:4-9

O God, as I come to Thee, I would find the moral way written into the essence of things, for I would offer my sex powers to Thee that Thou mayest use them for their best and highest purpose. I shall need wisdom, and I shall need power, for sex is very clamorous and often drowns out Thy still small voice. Help me. *Amen.*

Still My Urges with Thy Quiet
I Cor. 6:18; Gal. 5:16, 22-25; 4:19

God, my Father, here I come to offer Thee the turbulence of my urges. Still them with Thy quiet, direct them by Thy will, make them fruitful by Thy creative love, and lift them by Thy redemption. We must work this problem out together. For, apart from Thee, I can do nothing. *Amen.*

I Offer All Lesser Loves to Thee
Jas. 1:14-15; Prov. 23:7; I Cor. 7:1-2; II Cor. 5:14

O Christ, I would so fall in love with Thee and Thy ways that all lesser loves may become a part of that central controlling love. They shall lose themselves in Thee and find themselves in right expression. For Thou art the key to life—all life. I thank Thee. *Amen.*

No Comfort in Smoke
Hab. 2:5-7; Eph. 2:3; Gal. 4:9; 5:1

O God, I come to Thee for freedom. I do not want to be in bondage to a self-imposed craving, a slave to a thing. I want to depend for comfort, not on smoke, but on a Savior. I want my joy to depend, not on the most boosted brand, but on a quality—of life. Help me to shift my values. In Jesus' name. *Amen.*

Help Me to Cut Out All Parasites
I Cor. 6:12; 10:23-24, 31-33

My Father and my God, help me to be at my very best for Thee. This business of being a Christian is serious business and needs all my powers at their best. Help me then to offer them to Thee. Help me cut out all parasites that sap my strength and energy. For I have a race to run. *Amen.*

I Want to Be Ready
Eph. 5:16; Col. 4:5; John 9:4; Prov. 6:6
My Father and my God, I want to be ready
for the moment of my highest use, some great
moment that shall call for my best. Help me every
moment to get ready for that supreme moment.
Help me to be prepared, by getting ready every
moment. In Jesus' name. *Amen.*

May Our Disciplines Become Unconscious
Luke 12:31; 9:55-62; Matt. 5:29, 30
O Thou disciplined Christ, we would be like
Thee. Thy disciplines are so hidden, so much a
part of Thee, we can scarcely discern them. We
would be that way, too. May our very disciplines
become so naturalized within us that they become unconscious, and, therefore, effective. *Amen.*

Honest with Thy Honesty
Matt. 7:3-5; 6:24; Jas. 3:10-12; 4:8
O Christ, we do not see ourselves, for we look
at the sins of others with open eyes and then
turn a blind eye upon our own sins and weaknesses.
Help us to be as honest with ourselves as we are
with others—and more, help us to be honest with
ourselves with Thy honesty. In Thy name. *Amen.*

52

Drain Me of Insincerity
Phil. 1:10; Jas. 1:8; Acts 5:1-11

O Thou Crystal Christ, probe deep within my heart and find there the hidden infections of insincerity. Drain them to the last poisonous drop, lest they poison my whole system. Make me clean within of every hidden contradiction, for I want to be harmonious and effective. In Thy name. *Amen.*

A Self I Can Live With
Matt. 6:1-5, 16-18; 23:2-7

O God, I come to Thee with myself. I have tried to rationalize my insincerities and explain them away. I am through with explaining them away—I want them to be taken away. I want a self I can live with, and I cannot live with a self that is warring with itself. Then help me— and help me now. *Amen.*

This Three-Storied House Is Thine
John 19:38-44; 20:19-23

Holy Spirit, I see what I need; I need Thee. I need Thee, not as an occasional visitor with me, but as my constant Guest within me. This three-storied house of my body, mind, and soul is Thine. Take over charge. Put light and heat in every room, and let the light shine from every window— with no part dark. In Jesus' name. *Amen.*

Correct My Lopsided Virtues
II Pet. 1:5-9; Gal. 5:22-23; Eph. 6:13-17

O Jesus, so perfectly poised and harmonious, help my lopsided virtues to be corrected by Thy amazing balance and sanity. Where my virues have become out of proportion and have come to the verge of vices, give me grace to correct them— and the power. For my virtues must be redeemed, too. *Amen.*

Minds That Know, Wills That Obey
Jas. 1:5, 19; 3:17; Col. 1:9; Acts 6:10

O God, we hurt ourselves because we do not know Thy laws; and when we know them, do not obey them. Give us minds that know and wills that obey, and then we shall know how to live. We would know the truth and do it, and then we shall be free. Give us light and give us life, to walk in the light. *Amen.*

Wilt Thou Pass On Thy Health
I Thess. 5:23; I Cor. 6:19-20; II Cor. 4:10-11; 6:16

O God of my mind and of my body, I come to Thee to have both under the control of Thy redemption and guidance. May I pass on the health of my mind to my body, and the health of my body to my mind. But in order to do this, wilt Thou pass on Thy health to both my mind and my body. *Amen.*

Forgive My Sins Against My Body
John 10:10; II Cor. 12:7; Luke 13:11-17

My gracious, healing Father, I come to Thee with this body of mine. Forgive me for the sins I have committed against it and thus against Thee, its Creator. Help me to work with Thee to make it the perfect expression of Thy will. Give me insight into the laws of my body and help me to obey them when I see them. *Amen.*

A Mind-Purge for Body's Sake
Exod. 15:26; Ps. 103:3; Matt. 8:7; Acts 5:16

O God, I see I must be healthy-minded if I am to be healthy-bodied. Give me a mind-purge from all fears and worries and resentments, so that my body will be purged from all crippling disease and weakness. For I would be strong—strong for Thee. Make me the best that I can be. *Amen.*

No Alliance with Any Enemy
Ps. 26:1-2; Col. 3:5-7; Ps. 19:12-14

O God, I have faced my enemies, and in Thy name I have downed them. I thank Thee. Now help me to enter into no alliance with any enemy that pleads to stay. Help me to make a clean sweep. In Jesus' name. *Amen.*

Prayer—My Native Air
Jas. 5:16; Ps. 30:2; Luke 11:1; Ps. 27:14

Gracious Christ, teach me to pray. For if I fall down here I fall down everywhere—anemia spreads through my whole being. Give me the mind to pray, the love to pray, the will to pray. Let prayer be the aroma of every act, the atmosphere of every thought, my native air. In Thy name. *Amen.*

Body, Behold Thy Lord
Pss. 37:11; 119:165; John 14:27; 16:33

O God my Lord, my Life, I open every pore, every cell, every tissue, every artery, every vein, every bone to Thee. This body, in every part, is Thy temple—hallowed by Thy presence, cleansed by Thy purity, and taken hold of by Thy purposes. O body, behold thy Lord! *Amen.*

I Breathe Thy Calm
Pss. 37:1-11; 121

My Father, gently and quietly I breathe Thy calm and Thy peace into every portion of my being. My fever is gone in the great quiet of God. I am receptive in every fiber and every tissue. The healing of God goes through me, through me. I am grateful, grateful. *Amen.*

The Price of Thy Plan
Isa. 8:19; I Kings 19:12; John 10:4; Isa. 30:2
Gracious Father, Thou hast paid attention to the minute, fashioning the lowliest cell with handiwork; hast Thou no plan for me and my life? Thou hast! Help me to find that plan, to pay the price of working out that plan, and to make it the adventure of my life. In Jesus' name. *Amen.*

Thou Hast Set Us in Families
Eph. 5:25-33; Col. 3:18-19; Gal. 5:13-16
Our Father, who hast set us in families, and hast put us there to procreate the race, and to train us in the art of living together that we might make a Family of God out of the world chaos, help us to begin where we are. Help us to make the Kingdom operative in the little things of the home. Thus we shall be ready for the Greater Family. In His name. *Amen.*

Music Out of Misery
Isa. 37:3-7; 41:10, 13; 42:16
O God, my Father, I see I need not whine or complain. I can make music out of misery, a song out of sorrow, and achievement out of accident. I cannot be beaten. For everything is grist for my will. I will turn everything, good, bad, and indifferent, into something else. I thank Thee. *Amen.*

57

A Prayer for Youth
I Tim. 4:12; 5:1-2; Eccles. 12:1

O God, I am beginning this business of living in a serious way. I want a Way. I don't want to drift from wave to wave of meaningless emotion— I want a Way. If Thou, O Christ, art the Way, I will follow Thee through thick and thin, through popularity or through disfavor. I want a Cause— Thou art that Cause. I choose. *Amen.*

A Prayer for Middle Age
I Cor. 13:10-11; II Cor. 10:3-5; I John 2:14-17

My Father God, I am now getting to the time of life when the fires of life tend to burn low. Oh, don't let them go out within me. For if they die, then I die. As I go along I am gathering experience—help me to make that larger experience into fuller expression. Help me to grow in usefulness and power and love. I thank Thee that I can and will. *Amen.*

A Prayer for Old Age
Ps. 92:14; Acts 2:17

Gracious Father, help me to grow old gracefully and beautifully, to come to maturity majestically. Let me fill my mind and soul with Thee, so that when physical beauty fades, spiritual beauty may take its place. Physical beauty is an endowment; spiritual beauty an achievement—help me to achieve it by constant companionship with Thee. *Amen.*

Mastery over Money
Acts 20:35; II Cor. 9:1-15; I Cor. 16:2; Mal. 3:7-10; Mark 10:17-27

O God our Father, I am digging deep around the roots of my life. I am trying to tie up this root of money which is "a root of all evil." I cannot cut it entirely; but I can, and I do, tie it up so that it does not take too much nourishment from the soil of my life. I want to absorb it—I don't want it to absorb me. In Jesus' name. *Amen.*

Thou, Not Caesar, Art God
Luke 20:25; Acts 5:29; Matt. 22:36-40

Father, help me to get my values and my allegiances straight. I will give my loyalty to Caesar as long as it does not interfere with and contradict my loyalty to Thee. For Thou, not Caesar, art God. Help me then to fear no consequences of my loyalty to Thee, first, last, and always. *Amen.*

The Church—Thy Family
Col. 1:17-18; Acts 20:28; Eph. 3:14-15; 5:23-32

O God, I thank Thee that Thou hast a Family, and that I can belong to that Family. Make me a good member of that Family. May the Family spirit be in all I do and think and say. For I want others to love this Family. Help me to bring to the Family the constructive spirit of love and mutual aid. In Jesus' name. *Amen.*

A Prayer for the Church
Acts 2:46-47; 7:37-38; 16:5; I Cor. 16:19-20; Eph. 1:17-23

O God, I thank Thee that the Church has been "the mother of my spirit," the guide of my youth, the fellowship of my mature years—the home of my soul. May no class, no caste, no color lines mar the open fellowship of the Family. Help us to have a relaxed fellowship in which everyone will be at home—except those who sin against the Brotherhood. *Amen.*

Let No Hate Trouble Me
Luke 11:4; Eph. 4:32; Col. 3:13; Mark 11:25-26

O Christ, brand me deep. I surrender all hurts, all resentments, all retaliation. From henceforth I am free—free from corroding hate and cankering resentments. I shall love everyone—friend and foe—those who do me good and those who do me ill. By Thy grace I can do this, but only Thy grace. From henceforth let no hate trouble me. I bear Thy brand. *Amen.*

In a Dungeon So I Can See the Stars
Rom. 8:26, 28, 35-37; II Cor. 12:7-10

O Christ, Thou hast shown me how to take hold of the nettle of life when it stings, and make those very stings into sensitiveness to the hurts of others. I am plunged into a dungeon. Perhaps I am in this dungeon so that I can see the stars. For I know that nothing can defeat me if I remain undefeated within. I thank Thee. *Amen.*

Through Dungeons to Open Doors
I John 1:5-7; Acts 26:16-18; Jas. 4:6-10
O God, my Father, Thou dost make us go
through dungeons to open doors. How it must
wring Thy heart to have to stand aside and let
us fail! But Thou dost love us too much to let
us succeed on low planes. Precipitate the crisis that
we may go through the catharsis to the Resurrec-
tion. For we must be new—at any price. *Amen.*

A Brother of Men—Not a Brother of Class
Gal. 3:26-28; Matt. 9:9-13
O Christ, give me power to face soured, selfish
religion and to die for it, if necessary. For this kind
goeth not out except by prayer and fasting—
and a cross. Keep my soul from all interests of
class, from class thinking and class attitudes, and
help me to witness against them by word and
deed and attitude. Let me be a brother of men,
and not a brother of a class. *Amen.*

Help Me to Care
Matt. 5:43-48; Rom. 12:10, 14-15; 13:8; I John 4:7-21
O Christ, Thou didst care even when the multi-
tude sat in open-mouthed indifference and watched
Thee there. Help me to care like that. When everything I love is trampled on by indifferent feet,
help me to go quietly on to await Thy processes
of resuscitation. I can wait for Thee. *Amen.*

Break Race Prejudice on Thy Cross
Col. 3:9-11; Acts 10:34, 44-48; 11:12

O Christ, I thank Thee that Thou didst take all these racial insults into Thy heart and didst emerge out of that sea of hate the Son of Man, beyond race and beyond insult. Help me to do the same. Help me to identify myself with the underprivileged and the despised, and to take no privilege they cannot take. And perhaps the custom will be broken by that cross. *Amen.*

A Prayer for Group Decisions
Acts 15:22-31

O God, teach us how to come to a common mind. Help us to surrender the will to dominate. May all our decisions fit the pattern: "it seemed good to the Holy Ghost, and to us." May we be set to find Thy mind in every matter. In Jesus' name. *Amen.*

I Offer Thee My Hands
Acts 18:3; 20:34-35; II Thess. 3:6-10

O Son of a carpenter, and a carpenter Thyself, take away our false pride of being able to command the labor of others and help us to join Thee in making our communities places of health and beauty—veritable cities of God. Today I offer Thee my hands. *Amen.*

Let Recreation Be No Moral Holiday
I Cor. 6:9-10; I Tim. 4:8-12; II Tim. 2:22
O Christ, I come to Thee for guidance, for I want my recreations to be an integral part of my life for Thee and not a moral holiday. I submit all my recreations to Thee; cull out of them what is real and vital and let the rest be burned in the fire of my love for Thee. *Amen.*

A Christmas Prayer
John 1:14, 18; 14:8-9; Matt. 1:18-25
Gracious Father . . . May I *be* the Christmas message. *Amen.*

A Good Friday Prayer
John 15:13; Rom. 5:6-11; John 19:16-18
O Christ, I am bowed in the dust. If my sin is Thine, then how can I sin again? I will not. O Galilean, Thou hast conquered me. I cannot stand before this invading love. I bow forever at Thy feet. *Amen.*

An Easter Prayer
I Cor. 15
O Risen Lord, walk in the garden of my life, and then it will be forever dedicated—forever it shall be no place for sin. It is the place of life, eternal life. I am deathless, for my garden is the garden of the Lord. Life lives here. I thank Thee. *Amen.*

9 781432 588656

CPSIA information can be obtained at www.ICGtesting.com
Printed in the USA
LVOW08*0812160315

430725LV00014B/508/P